AT THE END OF TIME

Bishop Gerasimos of Abydos

AT THE END OF TIME:
THE ESCHATOLOGICAL EXPECTATIONS
OF THE CHURCH

Foreword by
Fr. Peter A. Chamberas

Holy Cross Orthodox Press
Brookline, Massachusetts

Second reprint, 2004
© 1997 Holy Cross Orthodox Press
Published by Holy Cross Orthodox Press
50 Goddard Avenue
Brookline, MA 02445

ISBN: 1-885652-06-2

LIBRARY OF CONGRESS CATALOGING–IN–PUBLICATION DATA

Papadopoulos, Gerasimos.
At the end of time: the eschatological expectations of the
church / Bishop Gerasimos of Abydos: foreword by Peter A.
Chamberas.
        p.   cm.
        ISBN 1-885652-06-2 (pbk.)
1. Eschatology.   2. Orthodox Eastern Church—Doctrines.
I. Title.
BT821.2.P33   1997
236—dc21   97-49366
                                           CIP

Contents

Foreword

After a lifetime of prayerful meditation upon the Holy Scriptures of the Church, His Grace Bishop Gerasimos of Abydos wrote this book on the eschatology of the Church – the "last things." It was a joyful experience to work with him as he developed the manuscript for publication. Unfortunately, he fell asleep in the Lord before it was ultimately published. However, as we worked on it he asked me to prepare this foreword and it is an honor for me to offer it in memory of this saintly hierarch.

Much that is written about the final events in the history of salvation is often marked by unbridled speculations, blind confessionalism, or naive romanticism. The reader of this book will find no such distortions or deviations, but rather a characteristic faithfulness to the spirit of the New Testament regarding the eschatological expectations of the Church.

The "last things" to take place at the end of time are by their very nature ineffable, too great and too glorious, to be dealt with adequately by our thought and our speech. In fact, the New Testament and the Holy Tradition of the Church exercise tremendous critical reserve and sobriety in discussing the eschatological expectations of the Church.

Faithful to this very spirit of the New Testament and the Holy Tradition of the Church, Bishop Gerasimos has prayerfully undertaken to help the faithful through this very important but difficult aspect of our Christian faith. In his characteristic way, Bishop Gerasimos has successfully put aside everything superfluous to emphasize what is truly important and necessary for the edification of the believer. He is not interested in critical arguments or in romantic speculations, but in the spiritual realities that have been revealed for us in the person and work of Jesus Christ and experienced in the Church. The profound reflections on Christian eschatology here, very artfully relate the future events to take place with the events which have already taken place in the ongoing history of salvation. For example, the Second Coming of Christ is understood and interpreted in the light of the first coming of Christ, the Incarnation and the entire divine plan of salvation. The Resurrection of Christ affirms the possibility of the future resurrection of all at the end of the world. The Final

Judgment is understood in the light of our present faith and life in Christ.

Moreover, the New Testament speaks of God destroying His world, bringing history to an end, and then recreating the world in a perfected, eternal and incorruptible form, precisely because God Himself created the world and man and set history in motion in the first place. To the fallen world of sin, corruption, suffering and death, God says an eschatological "No!" Then, He proceeds to make "all things new" (Rev. 21:5). We are reminded by Bishop Gerasimos that God's eschatological "No" has nothing to do with any negation of the physical world, any notion of escapism or other worldly romanticism. On the contrary, Christian eschatology expresses the infinite and abiding love of God, who must at last bring the world and mankind to perfection in His fulfilled and gloriously eternal kingdom.

We are able to look forward to this ultimate glory in God's eternal kingdom, precisely because "by his great mercy we have been born anew to a living hope through the resurrection of Jesus Christ from the dead." And not only this, but "an inheritance" is kept for us in heaven, "a salvation ready to be revealed in the last time" (1 Pet. 1:3-5). We have already received much in the Church, but we anticipate so much more in the future. All of Christian life in the Church is by nature intrinsically eschatological. That is to say, there is an abiding and unresolved tension between what is already a reality and a present experience in the Church and the future eschatological expectations at the end of time; between what has already been accomplished in Christ and what we as Christians are still anticipating. Christ has indeed come, but He will come again. The kingdom of God has been inaugurated, but its full power and glory will be revealed in the future beyond history. The ultimate act of God in history for the salvation of mankind has been consummated in Christ, but we still look for "a new earth and a new heaven." In Christ all of mankind has been redeemed, and yet we still expect an additional salvation, "a salvation ready to be revealed in the last time."

From the very beginning of the Christian era there has been an eschatological tension between the present and the future, between the "here and now" and the "not yet." The Church is living in two dimensions at once: the temporal and the eternal, the earthly and the heavenly, the militant and the triumphant, the historical and the eschatological. The work of salvation has begun, but it is still in progress. The Spirit of God has already come and is ever abiding in the Church, but the Church is still on the way, and the Christians are still pilgrims and strangers in this world, seeking the fatherland in God's eternal heaven. Christians live one aspect of their life in the Church struggling to conquer, and in the other aspect they live in the peace of victory; they pass one aspect of their Christian life here on this earth which will come to an end, and the other aspect they defer to after the end of time, when life will be completed and fulfilled at the Second Coming of Christ in God's eternal and glorious kingdom.

While it can be said that all of Christian faith and life is eschatological, Christian eschatology is, nonetheless, quite concrete in referring to the Second Coming of Christ or the Parousia, the final victory over Satan and evil, the Resurrection of the dead, the final Judgment of all, the new Creation and the eternal kingdom of God. These ultimate and final events at the end of time are the ground and content of our Christian hope, and they serve as a guiding and inspiring principle for the entire theological system of the Church.

In reflecting upon these eschatological expectations of the Church, Bishop Gerasimos has in mind, as always, the faithful members of the Church who need to be informed and guided through this difficult aspect of Christian truth. It is hoped that the light which shone through the life and work of Bishop Gerasimos, and which is reflected in this book will also shine upon his faithful readers for added enlightenment and edification.

Fr. Peter A. Chamberas

Introduction

Eschatology (from the Greek word ἔσχατον – *eschaton*, meaning the final or ultimate event) is the Christian doctrine concerning the last things, that is, the events that will occur at the end of time, at the end of present history as we know it. These events are the hopes of our Christian faith for the future and ultimate destiny of mankind and the whole world, when the kingdom of God will be fulfilled and perfected to its eternal glory (Rev. 22:5).

All men, philosophers and politicians as well as ordinary people, not satisfied with their present condition, live to some extent with a hope for a better future. Unable to break through and go beyond the bonds of the present form of the world, they expect these changes in life to come about within the present form of history. Christian faith and hope, however, has a spiritual vision of a real evolution in the history of the world. It envisions a radical change: the present history will come to an end and a new life, a new creation with a new heaven and a new earth will begin (2

Pet. 3:13; Rev. 21:1-5).

Hope is a basic virtue for man. It is a divine gift that provides consolation and courage in the struggle of life. In fact, Christian hope is numbered among the three cardinal virtues, the others being faith and love (1 Cor. 13:13; Col. 1:4-5). Faith and hope are of course inseparable. "Faith is the assurance of things hoped for, the conviction of things not seen." Faith makes our hopes certain, and hope in turn always nourishes faith and keeps it alive (Heb. 11:1-10).

Hope then is the breath of the soul; without hope you cannot speak about faith or religion. The faithful person lives with hope in the God of hope and love. He enjoys the good things in this life and runs the race of life with patience, seeking the "city which is to come" (Heb. 13:14). Hope for a future life in communion with our Lord and God is the most important element in our Christian faith. "If it is for this life only that Christ has given us hope, we of all men are most to be pitied" (1 Cor. 15:19).

Our Christian hope for the future is rooted in the mystery of divine economy, that is, God's plan for our salvation in Christ. To understand this mystery, one needs above all to have faith in God, a living God, the creator and sustainer of the world, a God who rules and guides history toward its final goal, toward the eternal life beyond death, beyond time as we know it, in the eternal and perfected kingdom of God. And no rational person can readily deny that a mind governs the world purposefully, when he sees in himself, who is a microcosm, a universe in miniature, that our invisible mind directs our whole life. Nor can one deny the continuity of life, since we believe that even in matter itself "nothing is lost," but only a mere change takes place.

Christian faith is of course also concerned about the needs of everyday life, our daily bread. Yet, it is especially applicable to spiritual things: faith in God, forgiveness of sins, and our salvation in Christ. Above all, Christian faith is hope related to the future: the heavenly blessings, the inheritance of the glory of the kingdom of God, and eternal life in a loving communion with God and one another. Christians, we can say, live with hope for the future. Our citizenship is indeed in heaven (Phil. 3:20-22). This present world is too small for us; we cannot be contained within this present world. We live and enjoy this present life with the love of God abundantly poured into our hearts through the Holy Spirit, and with certainty we expect the fullness of our life in the future, in the Parousia, that is, at the Second Coming of Christ (Rom. 5:1-11; 8:22-25; 1 Pet. 1:3-12; Heb. 13:14). In this present life we have only the first fruits, a foretaste of the future blessings. We expect to have in the future, in the ultimate consummation of all things in God at the end of time, the fullness of heavenly blessings. This is why St. Paul prays that God will enlighten the eyes of our hearts to know Him better and "what is the hope to which he calls you, what the wealth and glory of the share he offers you among his people in their heritage, and how vast the resources of his power open to us who trust in him" (Eph. 1:17-18; Rom. 8:18-26; Tit. 2:13; 1 Cor. 2:9; Col. 1:26-27).

Now and not yet. World history continues on its course toward its final goal, which is the completion of the kingdom of God, with Christ at the very center of history. The Jews lived with the expectation of the coming of the Messiah, the Savior of the world. For the Church the Messiah has already come. By His life, Christ has overcome evil, sin, death and the devil. Christ died and rose again and established a new life, a new creation. Christians live in this newness of life which is in Christ. They live the new life of the Resurrection. In the sacramental life of the Church, we experience this "first resurrection" (Rom. 6:1ff.), this spiritual regeneration.

While we live in Christ and in the Spirit now, we are still groaning for the fullness of our salvation, of our sonship in God (Rom. 8:18-30). Our Christian life is an ongoing race for fulfillment in the Church, which is the community of the "last times." The kingdom of God is ever being fulfilled in the Church and in the Holy Spirit.

This then is the ultimate goal of world history – the fulfillment of the kingdom of God. This goal and purpose of history gives meaning to our present life. Our life in the Church is lived here and now in the love of God, and with the certain hope that Christ will come again at His Parousia, when everything will be fulfilled – the Resurrection, the Judgment, the kingdom of God, and we will be with Him forever and ever. These spiritual truths have been revealed in Holy Scripture and will come to pass at the end of time. In the meantime, as faithful Christians, we live in hope, and especially in our life of worship in the Church we experience a certain foretaste of these future blessings now, even though they are not yet truly fulfilled.

The "Last Things" in Holy Scripture

All matters of religion appear difficult to most people because they are of a spiritual nature; but even more difficult is the topic of the "last things," for they have to do with future realities "that are not seen" (Heb. 11:1; Jn. 3:10-12), that only faith can "see," examine, and make real.

The Jewish people were the beloved people of God and yet they were not satisfied with their present life in this world. All the great personalities of the Old Testament lived with hope for the future, for the fulfillment of the promises made by God to Abraham. Their main hope was the hope of the coming of the Messiah–Savior, who would bring days of divine blessings for the Jewish people and for the whole world (cf. Lk. 2:25; 24:21). And they expected this to happen at some future date, in the last days of history – "in the last days," "in that day," "in the day of the Lord" – as this time was often referred to.

For Christian faith these ultimate and final events have a dual character. When we look

7

upon them from the perspective of the Old
Testament, the "last things" are realized in
the person of Jesus Christ who is the expected
Messiah. The entire history of Israel and of
the other nations had as its goal the coming
of Christ and the establishment of the Church.
All things in the history of Israel were types
(*typos* or signs) that became realities in the
person of Christ and in the life of the Church
(Jn. 3:14-16; 1 Cor. 10:11; Heb. 10:1; 1 Pet.
1:10-12). Indeed, all the hopes of Israel were
realized in the person of Christ and in the
life of the Church. With the movement of St.
John the Baptist, and especially with the life,
Cross and Resurrection of Christ, the *eschata*,
the new age began; the kingdom of God was
inaugurated. But from the perspective of the
Church, the "last things" in themselves are
expected to take place mainly in the future,
at the glorious Parousia, that is, at the Second
Coming, the future appearance of the Lord in
glory (Mt. 24:30; 1 Thess. 1:10; 4:16-18; 1 Tim.
6:14-15). It is then and there that we will have
the fullness of the eternal kingdom of God;
when we will experience a perfect *koinonia*
– communion with God in Christ, as our soul
yearns it. This is the height and the depth of
our faith and the wealth of glory that awaits
us (Eph. 1:17-18).

There is one world and its history is unified: from creation to the Incarnation, and through the Church to the Parousia, to the fullness of the kingdom of God. The Church lives between the first and the second coming of our Lord.

The Parousia and the End of the Age

The Parousia will take place in the final days, at the last stage of present history. With the Parousia we will also have the end of the present world and the beginning of the new one, the "new creation" (Rev. 21:5). From the old will come the new. This is the goal of the world, its perfection, its renewal and recapitulation in Christ. Thus the Parousia, the end and the goal of the world coincide.

The Parousia and the end of the world were a main concern in the days of the earthly life of Christ. Christ often pointed to the future for the consummation of all. He especially pointed to His future coming as the Son of Man, as the judge of the world (Mt. 16:27; 25:31; 26:64 Mk. 16:62; Jn. 5:28). The early Church lived with the expectation of His Parousia. A few days before His death, the disciples asked Christ: "When will this be, and what will be the sign of your coming and of the close of the age?" (Mt. 24:3). The first Christians lived with the hope of the Parousia, especially in view of the difficult persecutions in the early centuries, and they expected it to occur soon (Mt. 24:3-6, 34; Rom. 13:11; 1 Cor. 7:25-31; 1 Thess. 5:1-11; 2 Thess. 3:3-16; Phil. 4:5).

The Parousia and the Mystery of Christ

Belief in the Parousia of Christ completes the faith in the person of Christ and the mystery of the divine plan of salvation. With the ultimate event of the Parousia we have the complete truth about Christ and His work. The work of salvation is the work of God in Christ. It began with the Incarnation, the Cross, and the Resurrection, and is in motion towards its ultimate goal. The crucified and resurrected Christ is already the Lord. He has received every authority in heaven and on earth (Mt. 28:18-20), and invisibly, in the Holy Spirit, He reigns through the Church and guides the world toward the end – the perfection of the kingdom of God. The Parousia of Christ and our being gathered together with Him will be the final act of the divine plan for our salvation. With the Parousia the works of Satan, namely sin and death, will be completely destroyed. With the resurrection of the dead the kingdom of God will be perfected and the life of eternal blessedness will begin. This is the purpose of God's divine plan for our salvation. This is what the faithful anticipate.

The Time of the Parousia

We know well that the Lord will come again in glory (2 Thess. 2:2; 1 Thess. 4:11-17). The Church confesses: "He will come again in glory… whose kingdom will have no end." Christ gave us certain signs which will precede the Parousia (cf. Mt. 24 and 25). But these were given mainly to keep us vigilant in life. No one knows the precise day and hour of the coming of the Lord (Mk. 13:32; Acts 1:7).

At that time many curious people were making academic inquiries, as some do now, about the precise day of the Parousia. Some lost their patience and began to have doubts about the Parousia and the resurrection of the dead. Others believed that the Parousia had already come (cf. 1 Cor. 15:12; 1 Thess. 2:1-2). The Apostles, however, made it their purpose to assure us that the Second Coming of Christ as well as the resurrection of all the dead will take place, but in their own time (1 Cor. 15:23; 2 Pet. 3:8-13; Jn. 5:28f) .

Holy Scripture is not a scientific cosmogony, that is, a detailed account of the creation of the universe, nor a complete development of

human history. The Holy Bible speaks mainly
of the faith we must have in God and about
our relationship with Him. We cannot enter
into the details of the eternal will and plan of
God. We know God and His plans only to the
extent that they are revealed to us, and as they
are realized in history. And God has revealed
to us what is needed for our salvation. But we
shall see everything face to face when they
actually come to pass before us. Christians
must know now that Christ will come as king
and judge (Mt. 14:62). He will come at a time
when we do not expect Him. This is why we
must always be on guard, awake, and vigilant
as sons and daughters of the light and of the
day (Mt. 24:42; 25:13; Mk. 13:33-37; 1 Thess.
5:4-11; 2 Thess. 2:2; 3:11).

A Christian life is required of us, not curios-
ity about years and times "which the Father
has placed under his own authority" (Acts
1:7). We do not live our lives as Christians
out of fear that the coming of Christ is near,
nor because we hope to gain rewards. We are
Christians because we believe in the love of
God, and we live a life in Christ out of love,
being always ready to receive Him with great
anticipation. We are challenged to live with
the hope of the Parousia as did the early
Christians who prayed: "Maranatha – Come,

Lord" (1 Cor. 16:22; Rev. 22:20; 1 Pet. 1:3-12).
This is the way the early Christians lived their
faith in the Church. But do we today have
this faith and do we live with this hope? We
never have enough; we always need more
faith, more love, more prayer of hope: "Come,
O Lord..."

The "Last Things"
According to St. Paul

The New Testament does not present a systematic eschatology. It presupposes the general faith of the Church in the "last things," answering and emphasizing only questions that were raised in some churches at that time. The readers are left to understand these points within the full content of the faith of the Church. In order to formulate some idea about the "last things" it is necessary to keep in mind all the books that speak about this subject and especially the First Letter of St. Paul to the Corinthians and the Revelation of St. John. New Testament scholars prefer to research each book separately, but in this manner we are unable to reach a clear general conclusion because, as we have stated, the Apostles refer to only a few points which are to be understood within the general faith of the Church. The first New Testament writer that should be examined is the great Apostle to the nations, St. Paul, who has much to teach on the topic.

St. Paul speaks on the basis of belief in the resurrection of the faithful, a question raised by the Corinthians. He wants to assure the Corinthian Christians about the resurrection of the faithful that will take place at the Parousia of Christ. As St. Paul sees it, Christ was the first to be raised from the dead. Because of His life and His obedience to the will of God even unto death, Christ triumphed over the devil, sin and death, and was raised from the dead. Christ was "the first fruits of those who have fallen asleep," and in time these people will also be resurrected to life eternal. The resurrected Christ continues His work against evil invisibly in the Holy Spirit, in the Church, and through the Church. "For he must reign until he has put all his enemies under his feet. The last enemy to be destroyed is death" (1 Cor. 15:25-26). Christ reigns until every opposing power and authority in the world – evil, sin, Satan, death – is vanquished. The last enemy to be destroyed is death, and death will be destroyed with the Parousia of Christ in glory and the resurrection of the dead (cf. 1 Cor. 15:51-57). St. Paul speaks mostly about the resurrection of the faithful, "those who belong to Christ" (1 Cor. 15:23; 1 Thess. 4:14-18). Here he is not addressing himself to the resurrection of the unbelievers. He was dealing only with the question of the resurrection of the faithful and their "being with Christ." To this question St. Paul replies with the "yes" of the faith of the Church. The faithful will be resurrected and they will be resurrected at the Parousia of the Lord. St. Paul even speaks about the condition of the faithful who will be living at the time of the Second Coming of Christ in glory. "They too will be changed and will become incorruptible and thus all together we will meet the Lord coming in the clouds. Lo! I tell you a mystery. We shall not all sleep, but we shall all be changed... the dead will be raised imperishable, and we shall be changed" (1 Cor. 15:51-53). "For the Lord himself will descend from heaven with a cry of command, with the archangel's call, and with the sound of the trumpet of God. And the dead in Christ will rise first; then we who are alive who are left, shall be caught up together with them in the clouds to meet the Lord in the air; and we shall always be with the Lord!" (1 Thess. 4:16-17). This will be the revelation of the glorious freedom of the sons of God that is expected by the whole of creation (Rom. 8:16-25).

"Then comes the end, when He delivers the kingdom to God the Father... that God may be everything to everyone" (1 Cor. 15:24-28). The work of Christ was to destroy the forces of evil

and to bring all under His authority in heaven
and on earth. This will be accomplished by
our faith in Him and by a life like His. And
all this "to the glory of God the Father" (Phil.
2:6-11).

The end of present history and the work of
salvation in Christ comes with the destruction
of death and the resurrection of the dead.
At this point the kingdom of God is completed and the Incarnate Son now submits
Himself to God the Father; the authorized
Son–King delivers the completed kingdom
(the Church) to the one Godhead, "that God
may be everything to everyone," that God
may be everything for all people and all creation. The whole world, reborn, remolded,
reshaped and recapitulated in the person of
Christ, will be found in the love of God. There
will be one divine kingdom where the will of
God will prevail completely and where the
grace and the love and the light of God will
permeate all persons and all things. There, finally, Satan will be decisively and completely
destroyed (Rom. 16:20; Gen. 3:15; Rev. 20:10).
There will be no opposing power or energy
anymore against the plan of God and the
work of Christ, for the world will now have
become the kingdom of God. It is there that
the great ambassador of Christ, St. Paul, saw

with spiritual consolation the fulfillment of the divine plan of salvation. This divine plan for salvation began with the Incarnation, the Cross and the Resurrection, and continues in the Church until it is completed with the Parousia and the new creation. What the first Adam destroyed through disobedience, the last Adam, Christ, restored through obedience unto death, death on the Cross. Christ as the High Priest, through His sacrifice, purifies and sanctifies those who believe in Him. He makes them members of the kingdom of God and thereby leads the whole world to its ultimate purpose. This is indeed the purpose and the goal of the world. All persons and all things will be subject to Christ and through Christ to the one God, to the holy will of God, for God is in control of history, leading it to its ultimate purpose.

The submission of the Son to God the Father is not an act of servitude or of subordination, but of divine nobility. Submission to God the Father actually means that the Son has completed His special mission in the world. Mankind has been saved. The adversary powers have been destroyed and the whole world has been put under God. The perfection of the kingdom of God and the resurrection of the dead is the theme of St. Paul, and not the subordination of the Son to the Father. The Father was always king and the Son and Logos of God was always working together with the Father to bring about the kingdom of God (Jn. 5:17). But in the eternal will of God, the Logos also became man in the history of the world. In fact He became *Theanthropos,* God–man, without separating Himself from the Divinity, and He did this for the sake of man, for his salvation. This is precisely the depth of the mystery of Christ that surpasses all human understanding: It is not simply that divinity became humanity, but rather that God became incarnate in the second person of the Holy Trinity.

Christ is the eternal Son and Logos of God incarnate for the salvation of the world. His work is a work of God *ad extra,* outside of His divine nature. The kingdom of God will be still a reality *ad extra,* that is, an action of God outside of God's nature. The *Theanthropos,* the Son of God who became man, will act *ad extra,* as king and high priest and shepherd of His people forever. For they are indeed His people and He is one with them; He is the new Adam of the new humanity (1 Thess. 4:17; Rev. 22:5). In Christ, God came out of Himself to direct humanity to its ultimate destiny, to the kingdom of God.

The world will always be different and separate from the nature of God. And the Incarnate Christ will be the eternal king and high priest over the perfected kingdom that will never cease being the kingdom of God. There is only one kingdom of the Father and of His Son, our Lord Jesus Christ (Rev. 11:15; Mk. 13:41; Lk. 1:23; Eph. 5:5; 2 Pet. 1:11).

The triumphant Church in heaven will ultimately have its marriage with the Lamb, who is the Savior, Christ the God–man. And this marriage will not be a temporal one but eternal, and they will reign forever and ever (Rev. 21:9-11; 22:5).

A Double Resurrection?

In the phrase "Then the end will come..." some theologians seek to find a distinction between the resurrection of the faithful, "those who belong to Christ," and the general resurrection of all. According to St. Paul the end will come after the resurrection. This however will coincide with the delivery of the kingdom by the Son to the Father. And the delivery of the kingdom will take place when all the opposing powers against the will of God have been abolished, including death which entered into the world through sin. Death is abolished with the resurrection and the incorruptibility of mankind (1 Cor. 15:42, 51-57). Thus several events – the victory over the opposing powers, the resurrection of the dead and the delivery of the kingdom to the Father – are simultaneous. These events precisely constitute the glorious Parousia of Christ.

The Parousia, the resurrection, and the end are not separated in time but only in thought. There is no time here. The Parousia will take place at the end, when all the opposing powers, which Christ is combating now, are destroyed; when the kingdom of God is established. The final victory will be the victory over death that will take place with the resurrection of the dead and the immortalization of human nature. But this is precisely the goal of the world. Thus the Parousia, the end and the goal of the world are one and the same thing. The kingdom of God has been perfected in Christ. The world has reached the goal and purpose of its creation as the divine will of God had determined. Here then we have the desired end, the completion of the course of the world, and the regeneration, the beginning of the new age, the new creation, the eternal kingdom of God and of the Lamb, His Son. All of these events constitute the glorious Parousia of Christ (Mt. 25:31; 1 Thess. 4:16-17). Therefore, the resurrection of the dead, the Parousia and the end of the time coincide.

The "Last Things" in the Revelation of Saint John

The "last things" are presented somewhat differently by St. John in the Book of Revelation, the last book of the New Testament. St. John writes differently because he received the truth differently. He is not just writing a book based on certain sources. He writes what he has seen in visions or received through special inspiration. "I was in the Spirit on the Lord's day and I heard behind me a loud voice... When I saw him I fell at his feet... I looked, and lo, in heaven an open door! ... and lo a throne stood in heaven..." (Rev. 1:10-17; 4:1-3). Every vision stands for itself and has its own message. Through all of these images Christ speaks about the mysteries of God's will for the Church and the world (Rev. 1:1; 2:2-7; 5:1-5).

Exiled for the sake of the word of God to the island of Patmos, St. John, under the influence of the Holy Spirit, had visions in symbolic scenes which indicate, interpret and clarify things which are happening, or which are going to happen in the life of the Church (Rev.

1:1-11). In familiar images from the Old Testament, and from the current life situation in the Church, St. John saw and depicted for us the struggles of the Church of Christ against the manifold evils and the battles between the kingdom of God and the kingdom of the world. Behind the images of the beast and the prostitute woman, for example, are the persecutions by political and religious opponents of the Church, particularly the Roman Empire. Always hidden behind these opponents is the ancient serpent, the dragon, the devil, Satan himself, who deceives the nations and turns them against the Church.

The fundamental idea of the Book of Revelation is the belief that Christ is the Lamb, sacrificed for us. He who opens the seals of the book is the ruling king revered and worshipped by the Church in heaven and on earth (Rev. chs. 4, 5, 6, 12, 19). The Lord Christ, the sacrificed Lamb, leads the struggle with His armies – the Saints of the Church. Their weapon is their faith in the word of God to the point of self-sacrifice. The blood of the Lamb, the sacrifice of Christ on the Cross and His Resurrection strengthen them; the victory over the enemy is certain (Rev. 6:2; 12:11; 19:17-18). The Christology in the Book of Revelation, which emphasizes Christ as the sacrificial Lamb, is the most powerful witness for the power of the Cross in the salvation of the world, as the Church experienced it. The Cross, the Resurrection, the Parousia, all indicate clearly the absolute sovereignty of Christ (cf. 1 Cor. 11:26).

In chapter 1, St. John speaks about the origin of his revelation. The source of the revelation is God Himself, but it is Christ who, through an angel, reveals to St. John things which must shortly take place. Christ, the second person of the Holy Trinity, is always the mediator between God and the world. The Father *through the Son in the Holy Spirit* creates and saves everything. In chapters 2-3, St. John has visions on the contemporary spiritual condition of the Church in Asia. Christ exhorts the leaders of the churches to be steadfast in their faith and promises rewards for the victorious ones. These promises are mentioned throughout the whole book and especially in chapters 21-22. In chapters 4-5, St. John is in heaven in spirit and sees heavenly visions. We have similar visions in the Old Testament (cf. Is. 6:1f.; Ezek. 1:1f.; 2 Cor. 12:2-4). He sees the throne of God in all of its glory. Around the throne are twenty-four presbyters and four living creatures who represent the Church of the Old and the New Testament and the world, and they praise God the Creator. Between them and the throne stands Christ as the Lamb sacrificed, slain, for our salvation. The picture signifies the mystery of our salvation in Christ. At the right hand of God there is a book that is sealed with seven seals. No one can open, understand, or even look upon the book. Only Christ the Victor can open it; only the mystery of Christ can shed light on the mystery of the world. The book must symbolize the eternal will of God for the destiny of the world, and what is to happen to it, as St. John sees it in the Spirit in chapters 6-20. Christ who opens the seals of the book is the center and the ruler of history and the world. He lives and continues the work of salvation to the end.

The vision in chapters 4-5 is truly magnificent. God the creator and ruler of the universe is there in the brightness of the throne. Christ, through whom all things are created and through whom the plan of salvation is realized, is there as the Lamb slain for the salvation of the world. The entire Church and the whole world, in heaven and on earth, glorify God and the Lamb who was sacrificed for the sins of the world. God and Christ are inseparable and the Church glorifies them together (Rev. 4:9; 5:8-14). St. John has seen this vision on the "Lord's day" (Rev. 1:10), and chapters 4 and 5 have been considered as a prototype for the Divine Liturgy where the one Church of God lives the blessedness of salvation. In our worship, earth and heaven, time and eternity become one eternal present in the presence of God.

The magnificent vision which St. John saw in chapters 4-5 will be the main consolation for him and for the struggling Church and an assurance for the final victory. God and Christ are in control of history, and truth and love will prevail, while evil will finally disappear from the world (Rev. 20:10), and a new life will come to the world created and saved by God in Christ (Rev. chs. 21-22).

In chapter 6, Christ opens the first seal. St. John sees Christ as a magnificent victor. In the Book of Revelation, only Christ is the victor (cf. Rev. 19:11; Jn. 16:33). Here the first rider must represent Christ, the Church with the Gospel ready to face the other coming catastrophic riders, who represent worldly powers. This is the theme of the whole Book of Revelation: the struggle of the Church and its victory over evil by the power of the blood of Christ. St. John sees three other demonic powers, in opposition to Christ, that bring grief to the world and to the Church. He dramatically envisions the struggle between the Church and its enemies in the form of wars. Natural catastrophes are depicted as punishment from God for the enemies of the Church. The same theme, the persecution of the Church and the punishment of the persecutors, is repeated in chapters 8-19, with different images.

In chapters 6 to 18, Christ opens the seven seals of the book. In various symbolic scenes we see the fate of the Church in the course of the centuries. The history of the Church is a spiritual struggle for the cause of Christ, the fulfillment of the kingdom of God, the victory of good over evil on earth, of Christ over the Antichrist, the devil.

The army of Christ is made up of the saints of the Church, the believers. Their power is the faith in the blood of Christ; their armor is the word of God. The army of Antichrist is made up of the worldly powers, mainly the Roman Empire, symbolized by the two beasts and the harlot woman (Rev. 11:7; 13:1-17; cf. Dan. 7:11-12).

In spite of the harshness of the images, the entire Book of Revelation is written to provide consolation and encouragement to the faithful who are struggling to keep the faith in Christ alive, notwithstanding the great sorrow they are experiencing. After each persecution, the book presents an image of consolation for the faithful (cf. Rev. 7:9-17; 10:1-11; 18:20). These images are a confirmation of the victory of the Church. They comfort the struggling Christians and help them to be "faithful unto death" and to receive the crown of life (Rev. 2:10-11).

All of the events prepare and direct us toward the end, the Parousia of Christ. The Parousia is coming as judgment for the enemies of the divine plan and as a consolation and a reward for the struggling believers. The coming judgment is presented in the form of wars and punishment for the enemies, executed by God or Christ that leads to the final victory over Satan himself. There, we will have the end of the present plan of salvation, the end of the cosmic drama of history, and the beginning of eternal blessedness in the kingdom of God and of His Christ.

The final confrontation with evil is presented in chapters 19 and 20. In the pericope 19:11-21, we have a summary of chapters 6-18. The image is very powerful. Christ appears in His magnificence as King of kings, Lord of lords, and Judge of all. The war is waged by the beast and the false prophet. Both of these are organs of Satan, representing the political and religious authority of Rome (Rev. 13:1-18).

The outcome of the battle is prejudged. "And the beast was captured and with it the false prophet..." (Rev. 19:17-20). Thus the enemies of Christ and the Church were completely destroyed.

At this point the cosmic drama has come to its end; the hostile powers have been thrown into the lake of fire, and one would have expected the end, the Parousia. St. John, however, presents three additional scenes which end with still another direct confrontation with Satan and his final condemnation (Rev. 20:1-10).

In the first scene we see an angel binding Satan. In 9:1-2, we saw Satan falling like a star upon earth. The abysmal well opened up and various kinds of evil appeared. The abyss is considered to be the dwelling place of Satan (cf. Lk. 8:31). The angel binds Satan without resistance. This silent act itself speaks about the mysterious power of Christ over Satan (cf. Mt. 19:28-29; Jn. 12:31). In ch. 12:4-9, we see the first downfall of Satan. Satan lost, we might say, his battle on the heavenly plain by not succeeding in destroying the male-child that had ascended to heaven. (In the image perhaps we can see the birth of Christ and the persecution of mother and child by Herod in Mt. 2:7-18). This child is Christ who conquered

Satan through the Cross and who was resurrected and ascended to heaven, to God and
to His throne. This power of the Cross binds
and restricts Satan. And with faith in Christ
and in the power of His blood, the Saints are
victorious in their struggle against evil (Rev.
12:11). For the faithful, the devil is indeed
bound up. The grace of the sacrifice of Christ
on the Cross forgives and sanctifies the Saints,
unites them with Christ and makes them in-
vincible warriors of Christ against Satan (Rev.
12:11; Rom. 8:31-39).

The power of Satan is limited for one thousand years, that is, for a considerable period of
time. Numbers in the Book of Revelation are
always symbolic. Only God knows the actual
length of this period.

In another vision related to the previous
one, St. John sees the faithful in their blessedness (Rev. 20:4). The vision contains thrones,
and people are sitting upon them with the
authority to judge. Who exactly are the people
sitting, St. John does not tell us. In Rev. 4:4
the twenty-four presbyters, representing the
Church, sat on thrones. Something like this
had been promised by Christ to the Apostles
and to the bishops (Mt. 19:28; Rev. 3:21; 1 Cor.
6:2). More probably it refers to all the faithful
who have been liberated from the power of

Satan and who rejoice in blessedness.

"Also I saw the souls of those who had been beheaded for their testimony to Jesus and for the word of God, and who had not worshipped the beast or its image and had not received its mark on their foreheads or their hands" (Rev. 20:4). With a simple conjunction "also," St. John notes that in this vision he also saw the souls of the martyrs. (He does not say that those who sat on the thrones to judge were the martyrs, but that they were included there with the others). This indicates to us that the Church is really one of the living and of the dead, heavenly and earthly, triumphant and militant, one Church, all the believers united in a fulfilled and complete body, with a definite number – 144,000 sealed (Rev. 7:3-9; 14:3-5).

"And judgment was given to them." The vision does not say whom they judge and how they judge. It only presents Christ as an image of the Church. Judgment belongs only to God. The Christian does not judge anyone (Mt. 7:1; Rom. 14:4-5). Judgment rather will be according to our deeds. Christians can judge the world only by their good deeds (Mt. 5:14-16). The blessedness of the saints is judging and teaching the world, especially the enemies of the Church.

"They came to life (they lived – KJV) and reigned with Christ a thousand years," as long as Satan remained bound. Where they lived and where they reigned we are not told. What we can understand is that St. John saw the saints, the heroes of the faith, to be living and enjoying the blessedness of the kingdom of God; and for St. John all the faithful were martyrs-witnesses, as he himself was. We will see the blessedness in its perfection in Chapters 21-22.

"The rest of the dead did not come to life until the thousand years were ended" (Rev. 20:5). In this third scene, the other dead, that is, the souls of the unbelievers, in contrast to the souls of the saints, did not live during this period of time. They were not worthy to partake of the blessedness, a life in the presence of Christ. The unbelievers, even when they are alive are really spiritually dead (Rev. 3:1; 19:21; Lk. 16:23-26).

St. John calls this phenomenon "the first resurrection," a kind of resurrection before the general resurrection of all (Rev. 20:5-12). The text, however, does not indicate a resurrection; it only says that the souls of the saints were present and were taking part in the blessedness of the kingdom of God.

"Blessed and holy" are they who have a

part in the first resurrection. They are not afraid of the second death – the punishment in the lake of fire – which is the final separation from God and which will take place at the end of the millennium (Rev. 20:14-15). They have already passed the judgment (cf. Jn. 3:18; 5:24-29; 11:26). Those who live with Christ in the present life are not afraid of being separated from Christ in the Parousia (cf. Rom. 8:38-39; Phil. 1:23). "They shall be priests of God and of Christ, and they will rule with him for a thousand years" (Rev. 20:6; cf. 1:6; 22:5). This is the certainty of faith, that the now suffering Christians will for certain share with Christ the blessings of the kingdom of God for "a thousand years," that is, forever and ever.

The Millennium: The 1,000 Year Reign of Christ Before the General Resurrection

Revelation 20:4-6, the only text in the New Testament which speaks about the millennium, has created and continues to create problems for interpreters. Many interpreters, taking this passage literally, see that before the general resurrection the martyrs, the witnesses of the faith, will be resurrected to reign with Christ for one thousand years. After the one thousand years there will again be a great violent battle against the Church. At this time Satan will be destroyed and will be thrown into the lake of fire. After this the general resurrection of the dead will take place (Rev. 20:12-13).

The idea of a messianic interregnum existed among the Jews at that time, but in a variety of forms. St. John may very well have known about this particular idea. Some Fathers of the Church during the first two centuries believed in a millennium kingdom of Christ on earth, although this kingdom is always considered to have a spiritual character. The general conscience of the Church, however, condemned this idea of a separate millennium as incongruous with the general spirit of the New Testament and the experience of the Church that believes in one Parousia of the Lord in glory, in one resurrection for all the dead, and in one eternal kingdom of God and of Christ (Mt. 16:2; 25:31-46; Jn. 5:28-29; Rev. 20:12-13).

For the Church, the millennium is generally the Church itself from Pentecost to the Parousia. St. John, in one complete picture, sees the whole life of the Church under the protection of Christ, all the believers, alive or martyred, "living and reigning," enjoying the blessings of the kingdom of God, in contrast to and in spite of the affliction of the persecutions.

Because in our times many things are once again being said about the one thousand year reign of Christ on earth with the elect, and about the imminence of this reign, it is worthwhile to express a few thoughts on this subject. This is done not so much to give a definitive solution to the problem – for this subject will remain a mystery no matter how one actually understands it – but rather as an effort to understand the thought of the Church that has rejected this idea.

First of all, one may ask what possible meaning can a limited kingdom of Christ on earth have, particularly between two difficult struggles (Rev. 19:11-21; 20:7-10). What moral message is offered to the struggling faithful by a kingdom for only some of the faithful, the martyrs, at a time when all of us look for salvation and the eternal blessedness of the eternal kingdom of God, and particularly when we know that "with the Lord one day is as a thousand years and a thousand years as one day" (2 Pet. 3:8; Ps. 90:4). Another question is: What will be the destiny of the survivors on the day of the Parousia and the resurrection of the martyrs (cf. 1 Cor. 15:51-55; 1 Thess. 4:16-17)? Furthermore, if we take the passage as a historical continuity of the passage in Rev. 19:11-21, then one asks again: From where do the nations in the four corners of the earth come, since they were completely destroyed, and together with the beast and the false prophet (symbolizing the enemies of Christ and the Church) had been thrown into the lake of fire?

For a correct understanding of this passage we must keep in mind, first of all, that St. John is not writing a systematic history or eschatology of the Church. He simply sees certain images, which are complete in themselves, symbolic and prophetic revelations of the struggle of the Church, as it moves

toward its final goal – the Parousia and the
eternal kingdom of God. Secondly, the image here does not speak to us clearly about
an earthly kingdom. The phrase: "They came
to life (and they lived – KJV) and reigned" is
simply an absolute statement that does not
tell us anything about where and when and
how they reigned. Christ is not in the picture
on His throne as king. Those who appear in
the picture are presented to us as separate
categories that are linked by a conjunction.
As for the first category – those who sat on
the thrones – we are not told who they are.
Afterwards, with a simple conjunction "and"
(καὶ), the souls of the martyrs and confessors
of the faith are presented, but are not identified with those who sat on the thrones (cf. Rev.
12:14). When St. John says the souls, he does
this perhaps to distinguish them from the first
group which may be understood as living,
and to emphasize that even the departed ones
are sharing in the joy of the Church. Finally, St.
John adds for us another group of saints: those
who died or who are still alive, but who have
kept the faith in Christ and "did not worship
the beast," that is, the faithful who probably
did not witness with their life.

Thus we can conclude that St. John has, in
his visions, seen all the believers in Christ,

martyred, dead or living, without dividing them into classes, as rejoicing in heavenly peace in the blessedness of the kingdom of God.

The First Resurrection and the Second Death

St. John refers to the vision of all the believers rejoicing in the kingdom of God as "the first resurrection." But he does not present for us this most important event of the resurrection. The word he uses ἔζησαν – they lived (KJV) – does not necessarily mean resurrection. This indicates rather that his subject is not the resurrection of the martyrs, but the blessed life of the faithful, generally speaking. If it were a case of the resurrection, he would not see the souls of the martyrs but the martyrs themselves. Moreover, Rev. 20:12 does not indicate a first and second resurrection.

All of these points show us clearly enough that the text of Rev. 20:4-6, the only passage in the New Testament that speaks of a millennium, at least, does not oblige us to accept a separate first resurrection and a separate kingdom of Christ with the martyrs. One must really press the text to give us such a reading.

Because no one theory becomes necessarily acceptable as correct, I dare to express a few

41

additional thoughts on the subject, based always on the text as understood in the context
of the entire New Testament.

For a correct understanding of the passage,
we must leave the vision as St. John saw it to
speak to us by itself, as freely as possible, but
not independently of the other books of the
New Testament and the life of the Church in
which St. John lives and thinks. It is for this
living, militant Church that St. John sees the
visions. It is this militant Church on earth that
Satan is seeking to deceive and lead astray,
and it is for this Church that St. John is writing to comfort and encourage the suffering
people, and not for the perfected martyrs in
heaven.

First of all, St. John speaks in pictures, he
does not write a history of the Church. Rev.
20:1-10 must be seen as a separate section of
Revelation that presents synoptically in three
images the whole mystery of the work of
Christ. About this mystery the whole Book of
Revelation speaks to us, and with the events
of 19:11-21, the cosmic drama seems to have
reached its end. The enemies of Christ and
of the Church are destroyed. The scene in
19:11-21 may be understood as a conclusion
of what is dramatically presented in chapters
6-18. And it can be interpreted as an assurance

that the Gospel will prevail over the Roman Empire.

In 20:1-10, St. John sees the mystery of the Church in a different way. The vision is referred directly to Satan, who was hidden behind the beast and the false prophet. He is the deceiver of the nations who instigates them to war against the Church of Christ. Rev. 20:7-10 is the same as Rev. 19:11-21. The difference is that here Satan himself is uncovered and condemned to the lake of fire together with his cohorts (cf. Mt. 25:41). In Rev. 20:1-3, St. John sees that the authority of Satan has been confined. He cannot deceive the nations as he did before the time of Christ. This means that with Christ, His Cross and Resurrection, Satan is weakened and banished from his authority (Mt. 12:29; Jn. 12:31). Satan no longer has any power over the Christians who believe in the Cross and Resurrection of Christ; he cannot lead them astray. The deception of the faithful by the devil is a constant fear and concern through all of Revelation (12:8-12; 13:14; 19:20; Mt. 24:24). The battle is always won with the power of the Cross. The believers overcome evil by the blood of Christ (Rev. 1:5; 5:9; 12:1). Thus Satan is restricted and the Christians reign with Christ for a thousand years.

From this point of view, Rev. 20:4-6 is a

symbolic image, the most eloquent presentation of the eschatological expectations. It is a message of consolation and encouragement (for St. John and the Church that is still struggling), particularly after the harsh vision he had in Rev. 19:11-21. There are similar images of consolation in 7:9-17; 10:1-11, 18:20 and 19:1-10. In this image we should see the whole Church of the faithful, and not only the martyrs notwithstanding the great honor the Church has for them. The souls of those who were martyred, as well as those who bore witness to the word of God and to Jesus Christ are included. St. John cannot separate the Church into groups.

The whole Church as one, beyond time and space, is the one Church of Christ, existing from Pentecost to the Parousia. The Church in heaven and on earth and under the earth and in the sea is one and indivisible and complete, as indicated by the round symbolic number 144,000 (Rev. 5:13; 7:1-8; 14:1-14). All the faithful in the days of St. John were martyrs. St. John himself is sharing "the tribulation and the kingdom" (Rev. 1:9). All the faithful on earth or in heaven live and witness for Christ and constitute the one Church of Christ (Lk. 20:38; 2 Cor. 5:6-9; Phil. 1:21-23).

The First Resurrection

St. John sees the blessed life of the faithful and calls it the first resurrection, but he does not present us with the very important event of the general resurrection. According to the New Testament, there is no separate first resurrection; there is only the general resurrection of all, and the change of those who will be still living at the time (1 Cor. 15:51-57;1 Thess. 4:16-17; Jn. 5:28-29). The spiritual regeneration and blessedness of the faithful in Christ, however, may be called a first resurrection, a resurrection before the general resurrection. And in general, the New Testament does present the new life in Christ also as a resurrection from the dead. "When we were dead, (God) made us alive together with Christ... and raised us up with him... and made us sit with him in the heavenly place" (Eph. 2:1-6; Col. 1:13; cf. Rom. 6:4-11; 11:15; Gal. 2:19). He who believes "has passed from death to life" (Jn. 5:24). Christ said, "I am the resurrection and the life; he who believes in me, though he die, yet shall he live, and whoever lives and believes in me shall never die" (Jn. 11:25-26; cf. Mt. 8:22; Lk. 15:24). The faithful are already "a new creation;" they live the life of resurrection, but without implying an actual separate first resurrection.

The Second Death

By the same token the ultimate destiny of
the unbelievers in the lake of fire is called a
second death, without meaning literally a
second death. Thus we have a physical death
and a spiritual death, and we also have a spiritual resurrection and a physical resurrection,
which is the general resurrection.

The expression in Rev. 20:5: "The rest of
the dead did not come to life..." is probably
used to distinguish between the souls of the
martyrs and the souls of the non-believers. It
is a parenthesis to clarify that the blessedness
of the kingdom of God is a gift of God and is
given as a crown to those who struggle with
faith and love for Christ. This is clear for St.
John from the beginning (Rev. 1:5-6; 5:10).
The unbelievers and the cowardly have no
place in the company of the Saints and do not
enjoy any blessedness now nor in the future
age (cf. Rev. 21:7-8). This does not imply that
there will be a second resurrection for them.
Finally, the text does not say anything about
the living people at the time of the first resurrection and their relationship to the kingdom
of the martyrs.

Were they all dead? But then how is it that
we have another war in Rev. 20:7-10? Against
what church will this war be? The persecuted

Church must be the militant Church on earth.
This is the Church that Satan is always attack-
ing, not the Church of the martyrs in heaven. It
is difficult to imagine a war against those who
already have been victorious over the enemy
with their martyrdom. They are waiting for us
also to be perfected (cf. Rev. 6:9-11). Therefore,
we can conclude that the vision in Rev. 20:4
is general and absolute, and does not refer to
a certain place or time, to earth or to heaven,
to the present or the future. St. John lives in
the Spirit, in a semi-transcendent atmosphere.
With St. Paul he can say to us: "Whether in the
body or out of the body I do not know" (1 Cor.
12:3). Whether on earth or in heaven, whether
in the present age or in the future, I do not
know. Present and future, heaven and earth
are united for St. John and the Church (Rev.
5:13). Christ is now reigning (Mt. 28:18-20; 1
Cor. 15:25-28), and the Christians, together
with the souls of the martyrs partake of the
blessings of the kingdom of God. This is why
he can move so readily from the present to the
future, from the earthly to the heavenly, from
the blessedness of the faithful in the present to
the blessedness of the Saints in eternity. In Rev.
20:4, St. John has seen the one thousand year
reign as fulfilled and completed before his
eyes, and he says: "They reigned a thousand

years." In 20:6, where he sees the faithful in
eternity, beyond the general resurrection and
the second death, that is, after the millennium,
after the general resurrection and the second
death of the unbelievers, he speaks in the
future tense: "They shall reign," and uses the
same term as before – "a thousand years."

Therefore we can say that in this vision St.
John sees not so much the first resurrection nor
who is sitting and for how long, as he sees the
blessed state of the faithful, martyred and living. This is, after all, our theme here, namely,
the reign of the Saints. And they indeed reign
and judge the world with Christ the King
during these one thousand years, both here,
as long as the militant Church exists, and in
eternity. "Blessed is the kingdom of God now
and forever," we pray in the Divine Liturgy. It
is with the hope of the Parousia and the com-
pleteness of the kingdom of God that St. John
has written his book. The fullness of the blessedness we will see in chapters 21-22, where St.
John foresees the end as already come and the
one whole Church in its heavenly perfection,
as the Bride of Christ the Lamb. The kingdom
of God is one without subdivisions into persons and times. It begins on earth with faith
and the life of the faithful, and it is perfected
and fulfilled with life in heaven unto eternity

(Rev. 1:6; 5:10; 20:4; 22:5). And it is the faith, the love and the worship of God and Christ that must concern the faithful, and not *when* and *where* the kingdom will come, or for *whom* it will be, and for *how* many years it will last. For Christ is reigning now in the kingdom of God both in heaven and on earth (Mt. 28:18-20; 1 Cor. 15:25-28; Col. 1:13; Lk. 17: 20-21). The kingdom of God "is within us," and among us, and if we do not receive it and experience it here and now, we will most certainly not find it in the future. Personal experience here is essential. The suffering Christians lived by anticipation the blessedness of the kingdom in their present life. And it was the foretaste of blessedness and the hope of the Parousia that filled their hearts with joy and gladness, even during difficult persecutions.

This is the heavenly peace and blessedness of a life in faith and love in Christ. If we do not feel this blessedness in our hearts we are not yet Christians; Christ does not yet really live in us (Gal. 2:20).

The Final Victory Over Satan
(Rev. 20:7-10)

"And when the thousand years are ended, Satan will be loosed from his prison..." Satan has been confined by the power of Christ, and the faithful reign with Christ for one thousand years – regardless of how we understand this period of time – referring only to the martyrs or to the life of the Church in general, from Pentecost to the Parousia, to the close of the age (Mt. 28:20). Yet evil still exists, and all Christians are fighting, pressing on "for the prize of the upward call of God in Christ Jesus" (Phil. 3:14), that is, for the resurrection and for Christ Himself. Satan is not to be completely destroyed during this time. And at the end of this period he will again be free to deceive the nations and turn them against the Church. This battle will be a difficult one, the final effort of Satan to halt the work of Christ. It will be reminiscent of the fierce war of Gog as the Jews knew it from Ezekiel 38-39. Christ too predicted fierce persecutions just prior to the Parousia (Mt. 24:6-14; Mk. 13:8-20). Now, St. John, who is in exile when he sees and writes these things, knows and experiences first hand the wrath of Satan.

The Antichrist

We do not know if this will be some particular persecution or the climax of the opposition to the Church in general during the last days. Here in the fearful Gog of Magog we must see the Antichrist whom we have already seen in chapter 13. He is a man, identified with the cryptic number 666. (The faithful of that time who were expecting the appearance of the Antichrist must have known something more about this name). For St. Paul the Antichrist is the man of lawlessness, the son of perdition, who does not respect God and wants to sit himself upon the throne of God. The greatest sin for man is the will to usurp the throne of God, to defy God, to take the place of God. The lawless one will appear with satanic activity and power to deceive those who find pleasure in falsehood and unrighteousness, and do not love the truth of Christ in order to be saved. Such is the Antichrist who will fight with satanic ruthlessness against the Church, as did Gog of Magog (cf. Ezek. 38-39; 2 Thess. 2:3-12; Rev. 13:5f). The Antichrist will be destroyed by the Lord Jesus "by his appearing and his coming" (2 Thess. 2:8). Who is the

Antichrist? Basically, he is the devil, but also he is every person who is against the work of Christ for our salvation (cf. Mk. 8:33; 1 Jn. 4:2-3). "If you see a person opposing God, he is the Antichrist." At every difficult moment of history people seek to see the Antichrist. Today enough powers are working against the will of God, against religion. We cannot know, however, when the time of the real Antichrist will be (cf. 1 Jn. 2:1-8).

The strange thing is that all the civilizations have developed from some religion, and particularly from the Christian religion. Now that we are more civilized, many people tend to deny the power of religion; they become secularists or agnostics, or are simply indifferent to religion. They may also attack religion as being hostile to them or to their way of life. Man, moreover, wants to exercise his power independently of God. He even makes laws to protect his independence from every religious ideology, and does not see that this independent power leads him to destruction.

In 20:9-10, St. John sees that "they marched up over the broad earth and surrounded the camp of the saints and the beloved city" (Rev. 20:9), that is the Church, the new Jerusalem, the new Israel. The perfect Jerusalem will come down from heaven, from God (Rev.

21:1-11). The war itself is not described. It is essentially spiritual warfare and not an "atomic" war. In any case the victory is here again certain as in Rev. 19:11-21.

"But fire came down from heaven and consumed them..." The Church was saved by the fire that came down from heaven. The devil who directs all the anti-Christian activities was condemned to eternal punishment in the lake of fire and sulfur. His cohorts are also there, and all the opponents of Christ, even death itself, will also join them there (Rev. 19:20; 20:10-15). This then will be the final battle against Satan who is the cause of all evil. This is the climax of the war against evil that started at 6:1. Is this a sign that evil will exist to the very end of this world, allowed by God as a test to our faith, and perhaps only God will put an end to it when the fullness of the time comes?

Why Satan will be granted freedom again belongs to the mystery of the fall of man and the mystery of divine providence for salvation. Perhaps we ourselves let him loose by our own lack of faith and love (cf. Mt. 24:10-12). If we believe the one thousand years to be the time of the life of the Church from the Resurrection to the Second Coming of Christ, then we can more easily understand that toward the end of history Satan will increase his efforts against the Church. "He must be loosed for a little while" (Rev. 20:3), perhaps to test our faith and our commitment to Christ. He will even attempt to deceive the elect (Mt. 24:8), and will deceive many even to "worship the devil."

Why does fire fall from heaven? This too is a mystery. This is how Ezekiel also saw it (38:18-23). Fire is a way of purification but it is also a way of judgment. The lesson of course is that in the world there is a moral order. Evil does not belong in the world as created by God, and evil will eventually be terminated and will disappear. God will put an end to evil from above, as redemption itself comes from above, from God Himself. This will be done as God Himself chooses and wills. Everything in the world is subject to God. If the purpose of God does not succeed within history, the God of history puts an end to the cause of failure and begins a new history. The new creation in Christ through the Incarnation, the Cross and the Resurrection is a new history within history.

With the condemnation of Satan and all the enemies of Christ and of death itself, we have the end of the present world. We also have the resurrection, the judgment, the *paligenesia* (the regeneration) and the eternal kingdom of God. This is how St. Paul also envisioned these things (1 Cor. 15:20-28, 51-58). All of these things constitute the glorious Parousia of Christ, His Second Coming in glory. All Revelation looks forward to this end, to the marriage of the Lamb (Rev. 19:7; 21:1-4; cf. Mt. 22:2-14).

The Parousia

In the New Testament, the Parousia is presented in the images of the Old Testament and Jewish tradition. The final trumpet of the Parousia will sound and with it Christ will come down – as He ascended before – and the dead will be raised first. Then those who are alive will be changed and all together they will be caught up in the air to meet Christ coming in glory in the clouds (1 Thess. 4:13-18; Jn. 17:24; Acts 1:9-11). This will be the regeneration and the renewal of the whole world, the new creation, life eternal. This is the hope of faith, and this is what the whole world is anticipating (Rom. 8:19-25). This is the "evolution" in which the Church believes. Life and history are not a cyclical repetition, but a direct line of movement from creation to eternity; from creation in Genesis to the new creation in the Book of Revelation. This is the ultimate destiny of the world, and it is at this point that we will hear the final "It is finished," that is, the divine plan of salvation is now fulfilled (Rev. 21:5).

The Resurrection (Rev. 20:12-13)

The Resurrection is the most important aspect of Christian eschatology. The resurrection of the dead is the main hope of the Gospel. Christ preached the resurrection with certainty (Mt. 22:29-33; Jn. 5:29), and He confirmed it in action with His own Resurrection. This is the reason why the Resurrection of Christ, the empty tomb, and the appearances of the resurrected Christ to His disciples constitute the heart of the Gospel (Mt. 28:6; Mk. 16:6-7; Lk. 24:13-53; 1 Cor. 15:1-11). The phrase, "I have seen the Lord" resurrected, is proof of the authenticity of the Apostle (1 Cor. 9:1; 15:8; Jn. 20:18-29; Acts 1:22). Without the empty tomb of the Lord and the hope of the resurrection of the dead, one cannot speak seriously about the Christian faith. If Christ was not resurrected, then neither will the dead be resurrected. And if the dead are not raised, then the Christian faith is in vain, and we are found to be false witnesses of God. If hope in Christ was based solely upon this present life, then Christians would be the most pitiful people on earth (1 Cor. 15:17-19), particularly in view of the persecutions suffered in the past and those that many suffer even today.

The experience of faith, however, says: "... But in fact Christ has been raised from the dead, the first fruits of those who have fallen asleep" (1 Cor. 15:12-20). Christ was raised from the dead and His Resurrection is a confirmation and guarantee of our own resurrection. The same God "who raised Christ Jesus from the dead will give life to your mortal bodies also through his Spirit which dwells in you" (Rom. 8:11). "We declare to you by the word of the Lord, that we who are alive, who are left until the coming of the Lord, shall not precede those who have fallen asleep. For the Lord himself will descend from heaven with a cry of command, with the archangel's call, and with the sound of the trumpet of God. And the dead in Christ will rise first; then we who are alive, who are left, shall be caught up together with them in the clouds to meet the Lord in the air, and we shall always be with the Lord." (1 Thess. 4:16-17). (The dead will rise first because it was for them that the question of resurrection was raised. The living hope to see the Parousia of Christ in their own lifetime). And the Church confesses: "I expect the resurrection of the dead and the life of the age to come."

St. John himself sees prophetically and describes the event of the resurrection as realized
before his eyes. "And I saw the dead, great
and small, standing before the throne... Death
and Hades gave up the dead in them..." (Rev.
20:12-13). He does not put the martyrs into a
separate category here, nor does he mention
the living (1 Cor. 15:51). He just sees the event
of the resurrection.

The human mind cannot comprehend the
mystery of the resurrection. Therefore, many
people do not take the resurrection seriously
and literally. Only with faith and revelation
can we speak about resurrection, and this as
a religious experience, a vision and an inspiration.

To believe in the resurrection we have to see
the whole world with the eyes of faith and in
its deepest mystery. We need to acknowledge
its relation to God the creator and the place
of man in the world, but not as a mere object
for chemical and mechanical examination
and exploitation. Man was created from the
dust of the earth, but he is not merely dust.
We cannot limit man to be simply just a part
of this world. He is a unique creature of God
who partakes both of earth and of heaven. According to revelation, man was created in the
image of God, a creature somehow similar to

God, destined to live in communion with God
and to strive to reach even the likeness of God.
Man is to rule the world, to enjoy the goods
of the earth and to praise God his creator. The
world was created for man, that he may take
care of it but not to destroy it.

Death was not in the original nature of
man. It was introduced to the world by the
sin of man. "God did not make death... God
created man to be immortal... in the image
of his own eternity. It is through envy of the
devil that death came into the world (Wis.
Sol. 1:13; 2:23).

Sin has disturbed the relationship between
God and man, introducing death into the
world. Man, however, is always looking beyond death; his soul is longing for God, for a
life in communion with the eternal God. Man
was created from the dust of the earth but was
not meant to return by death to dust. Man
received in himself the breath of God and is
destined to reach the likeness of God, to live
in the life of the eternal God. "In him we live
and move and have our being" (Gen. 1:26-29;
2:7; Acts 17:26-28).

Christ as man always lived in permanent
and perfect communion with God the Father
(Jn. 4:34; 8:16-29; Heb. 10:9-10). Through His
faith, obedience and sacrificial love, Christ

overcame sin, destroyed death by His death and, through His Resurrection, opened the way for our own resurrection and ascension to God the Father (Jn. 14:6; 2 Cor. 4:14; Eph. 2:6; Phil. 3:20). Christ is the "resurrection and the life" for us all (Jn. 11:25; 14:6). Thus, for the believer life is not a movement to decay and death, but a movement to fulfillment and completion. Natural death is not the real end of life but the gate to enter the real life in perfect communion with Christ and God (Jn. 5:24; 14:3; Phil. 1:23; Lk. 23:43). We experience a foretaste of this new life with Christ in our present life (2 Cor. 5:1-8). In the resurrection we will have it in its fullness, in perfect communion with Christ our Lord, rejoicing in His glory forever (1 Jn. 3:1-2; 1 Phil. 3:21; Rev. ch. 21-22). There will be no more sin, pain, corruption and death, but life in the kingdom of God forever and ever. It is for this life that we are created from the beginning.

Therefore the resurrection is certain. The Church believes steadfastly in the resurrection of the dead. This means a resurrection of bodies and not simply an immortality of the soul, as the ancient Greeks believed and as many people in the world today believe. At His Incarnation, Christ assumed a human body. He sanctified it, He deified it, He resurrected it, and in His resurrected body He ascended into heaven and sat at the right hand of God. He will come again with His body in glory, and people will be able to see "the one they have pierced" (Jn. 19:37; cf. Mt. 24:30). The whole man consists of both body and soul. Man lives with a body, and with the body he will be judged for whatever good or evil he has done (2 Cor. 5:10). Man exists as soul and body. The spirit of man expresses itself through the material body. The spirit uses the body and, with its expressions, the body becomes the visible sign of the invisible spirit. This is the dynamic of human nature. Man is becoming what he is destined to be by his creation in the likeness of the eternal God, who is spirit.

How the resurrection will take place will remain a mystery. It belongs to another world, a world different from the one we live in now.

St. Paul gives examples from nature which witness to a type of resurrection, because he wants to show us that God has the power to resurrect us and to give us whatever type of body He desires (1 Cor. 15:35-44; Jn. 12:24). Even those who will be living at the time of the Parousia will be changed in body and will become a new creation. The corruptible must put on the incorruptible and the immortal.

The kingdom of God is incorruptibility and immortality. The corruption of fallen man cannot inherit incorruptibility (1 Cor. 15:50-57). St. Paul imagines the resurrection as a new spring. A new life blossoms from the death of the old (1 Cor. 15:42-44). The dying seed becomes a tree, and the dormant silkworm is transformed into a beautiful butterfly. These are two examples of this truth in nature. The body of the resurrection will, in any case, be different from the earthly body, but also similar to the glorified body of Christ: incorruptible and immortal, angelic and spiritual. It will be conformed to our spirit (1 Cor. 15:35-57; Rom. 8:29; Phil. 3:21). It will be an appropriate instrument for the spirit to express itself. There the human person will find his and her completion. For the Fathers of the Church, the resurrection is the restoration of human nature to its pristine glory. The seed becomes a tree, the silkworm becomes a beautiful butterfly, and the rosebud opens out to a full and glorious bloom.

The Final Judgment
(Rev. 20:11-15; Mt. 25:31-46)

Together with the resurrection will occur the general judgment. Parousia, resurrection, judgment and new creation come together. Time will not exist as we know it. Eternity begins and everything takes place "in a flash of an eye" (1 Cor. 15:52). In speaking of the Parousia, resurrection, judgment and new creation, we must not forget that we are speaking in human terms about divine actions and realities.

The vision of the judgment reassures Christians about the existence of justice and the restoration of the moral order. Judgment comes as a consolation for the righteous, and as a dreadful threat for the wicked. The description of the final judgment is brief and simple, while imposing. The throne of judgment is glorious, great and brilliant, just like the Judge sitting upon it. The throne is the symbol of the divine presence. We do not see the Judge, only his great glory. Before the great brilliance of the Judge, it appears as if earth and heaven disappear. The old things pass away to become new (2 Cor. 5:17). The people however remain. Everyone stands before the white throne, accountable before the living God. At the calling of the Judge, the dead rise up. The sea, the earth, and Hades give up the dead they are holding. The book is opened and all, great and small, are judged according to their works. Man himself creates his future with his faith and his works. There is a separate book, the Book of Life, which emphasizes in particular that judgment and salvation is based on our faith in the person of Christ. Those who are not recorded in this book are those who did not believe in Christ the Savior and did not live a life according to the will of God. These are thrown into the lake of fire. In this same lake of fire the devil and death and Hades are also thrown (cf. Rev. 22:10; Mt. 25:41). What this lake of fire is, we do not know. The event itself is called "the second death," the spiritual death, the eternal separation from God, who is the source of life. The first death is physical death and all of us will die this death. The second death is the condemnation which comes according to the works of each person. This second death has no power at all over those who are written in the Book of Life, who believed and lived in faith, those who experienced the "first resurrection," who experienced the blessedness of the kingdom of God in this life. These will never be separated from God and Christ. In fact death only brings them closer to Christ (Phil. 1:23; Rom. 8:35-39; Rev. 20:4-6; cf. Jn. 3:18; 5:24-29; 11:25-26; 14:30).

The Judge

St. John does not name the judge sitting upon the throne of judgment. He could not see him – who could see God (Ex. 33:18-23)! God is invisible as Judge in His glory. He only speaks and acts from the throne (Rev. 21:3). St. John only presents the judgment as an event. The essential meaning of the passage is that the judgment will indeed take place. The details are not his main interest.

According to St. Matthew, Christ will judge the world (Mt. 16:27; 25:31). But according to St. John, God the Father judges the world through the Son (Jn. 5:22-30; cf. Acts 10:42; 17:31). The title of Christ as the Son of Man implies His office as the judge of the world (Jn. 5:27). The Son of God who became man will judge men, but the faithful together with Him will also judge the world by their faith and life (Rev. 3:21; 20:4; 1 Cor. 6:2).

Does God judge? All of us approve of judgment and justice, but we prefer that it be applied to others. Because we all fall short, no one really desires judgment for himself. This is why many raise the question: "Is it possible for the good God, who is Love itself, to judge the world and particularly to condemn people to eternal punishment?" Christ Himself said: "God did not send the Son into the world to judge the world, but that the world may be saved by him." God indeed does not judge, but loves and saves. "For God so loved the world that he gave his only Son, that whoever believes in him should not perish, but have eternal life" (Jn. 3:16-18). The very heart of the Gospel is that "God is love." And yet there will be judgment and God will judge the world through the Son. Or, rather, the people will judge themselves by their attitude toward the person of Jesus Christ. Christ judges with His word and work because the word and work of Christ is the word and work of God for our salvation. God acts in Christ. "In Christ, God was reconciling the world to himself" (2 Cor. 5:19-21). This is our faith. Whoever believes in Christ is saved and avoids the judgment. Whoever does not accept Christ does not accept the Father and is consequently judged (Jn. 3:18-36; 5:24; 8:15-18, 28-29; 10:30; 12:44-50; 15:23). Christ came into this world as light that brings life. He was light in His life and through His life He is now giving life to the world. In Christ, God is always working as light to bring life to the world. Where there is light there is also life. Where there is no light, there is no life but only darkness and death. We see this even in our days with the darkness and the death that is so prevalent in our city streets.

Christ is the light of the world. "And this is the judgment, that the light has come into the world, and men loved darkness rather than light..." (Jn. 3:19; 1:5). Everyone, Christians and even non-Christians, recognize that Christ with His word and His life is the light of the world. And yet many do not accept Him as the light of their life, as Savior and Lord. They do not accept Christ as light because they approach Him "according to the flesh" (Jn. 8:12-19). They approach Christ with human knowledge and rational proofs. Human knowledge however is poor, limited and cannot give us a personal God. God who is known by the mind is not God, but an idol. He is a God created according to the image of man. He is not God the Creator and Father who cares and does everything for our salvation (Jn. 3:16).

God is known and approached only to the extent that He reveals Himself to us. And the highest revelation of God we have in the person of Christ – a revelation in a person, not only in a word through the prophet. God is known only in Christ and Christ is known only through the Father. "He who has seen me has seen the Father." "I and the Father are one" (Jn. 14:9; 10:30). The revelation of God is one. The Father witnesses to the Son and the Son witnesses to the Father.

"No one knows the Son except the Father, and no one knows the Father except the Son and anyone to whom the Son chooses to reveal him" (Mt. 11:27). Son and Father are known and recognized mutually. If we do not recognize God as Creator and Father, we cannot believe in Christ who suffered out of love for us. And if we do not believe in the Son, we do not know the Father, because only in the Son, and especially in His Cross, have we seen the Father as love. "No one has ever seen God..." Only the Son who is one with the Father has spoken to us about the Father (Jn. 1:18; 17:1-8; 15:22-25). Only in the Incarnate Christ can we see and worship the invisible God.

Thus indeed there is a judgment because there is a moral order in the world. God will judge the world in Christ, or rather the world is judged before God by the position it takes regarding the light and the truth of Christ.

The kingdom of God is a kingdom of free men and women, and it is built on Christ our Savior and Lord, with the cooperation of free people. In faith and love, we all have to build ourselves upon Christ the cornerstone to become a living spiritual house, a dwelling place of God. Man is free, lord of his destiny. In this freedom his position in eternity is judged. Free man determines his future for himself. God does not force us to love Him. He respects the freedom with which He endowed us. We may choose to deny Him. But all of us are responsible for the role we will play in our life. One will either believe in the light and become a son or daughter of light and have eternal life, or he or she will reject the light and will be in the darkness of life, far from the light of life eternal. And far from the light there is no life, only hell, no matter how one thinks about it.

Why man, who wants light, does not accept the light of God remains one of the mysteries of the freedom of man. Concerning this difficult question, Holy Scripture always refers to Isaiah 6:9 to find some answer (cf. Mk. 4:12; Jn. 12:40; Acts 28:26). The kingdom of God is the kingdom of love and light, and it is built by those who believe in the light and who seek to become sons and daughters of the light, and who bear witness to the light by their very lives (Mt. 5:14). Paradise is to be in the love of God, to have communion with God. Hell is the repudiation of the love offered to us by God; it is separation from God. Our problem is that we do not take our faith in the living God seriously. We reduce God to a simple theoretical notion or idea which does not demand our obedience. "And all were judged by what they have done... and if anyone's name was not found written in the book of life, he was thrown into the lake of fire" (Rev. 20:13-15), to be tormented forever and ever (20:10; Jn. 5:29; Mk. 9:43).

Apokatastasis (Restoration)

The human heart and mind cannot easily accept that a loving God could condemn people to eternal punishment and damnation. Therefore, from the beginning there appeared here and there men of the Church who have thought of the possibility that this punishment might end. The fire is there for only a limited time as a means of purifying the soul (1 Cor. 3:13-15; 1 Pet. 1:7; Rev. 3:18).

The idea is expressed as a *theologoumenon,* (a debatable theological issue), and was never accepted as a dogma of the Church. The idea is appealing to the Christian heart of love, but it cannot have a real meaning. It just adds another period of time of preparation after death and even after the resurrection, which is not indicated in the Holy Scriptures. The Scriptures speak about punishment or destruction, and indicate this present life as the period of preparation. Even if we accept punishment just for a certain time only, it still will be a hard punishment. Our mind and heart cannot be the measure for the acts of God. We cannot, of course, know exactly about the life in the hereafter. Nor do we know what this condemnation really is. We cannot speak theoretically on these important things. We speak only on the basis of revelation and the vision of great persons of faith, who are interested in the positive things concerning our salvation. The Church Fathers do not take the idea of punishment literally. They understand punishment as the deprivation of divine light and life. God does not punish anyone. He only loves and saves. God is love and He invites us to live with Him and have life in abundance (Jn. 10:10). We, however, are free to accept God's invitation and follow Him, or to go away from Him. Paradise is a life with God, feeling at home with God; a life in communion with God and with each other in love and peace, and in an ever increasing share in the grace, glory and life of God. Damnation, on the other hand, is a life without God, peace and love; it is a state of being lost and starving in a country far away from God. But this cannot satisfy and appease our loving heart which longs for God.

St. Paul speaks about the general restoration of all, but he does not say how one will be subjected to Christ and through Christ to God, "that God may be everything to everyone" (1 Cor. 15:28). We do not know whether the hostile powers will be changed, healed, forgiven or destroyed in the lake of fire. St. Paul always speaks for repentance in our life here and now and never after our death.

Therefore it is better to avoid discussing the negative side of condemnation or punishment and to concentrate on the positive side of our salvation. It is for our salvation that our Lord became man. The Gospel was written for our salvation, not for us to learn who will be saved and who will be condemned. Let salvation be our concern and effort. That, after all, will be our real joy, "that our names are written in heaven" (Lk. 10:20; Jn. 20:31).

The New Creation (Rev. 21-22)

"Behold I make all things new..." (Rev. 21:5)

With the final condemnation of evil, the resurrection and the judgment, the end of the present world has come and the new one begins. This is what the Church expected from its very beginning. The throne of God appears in all its brilliance, and before the face of God the earth and heaven disappear. As the doctrine of the Church teaches, earth and heaven are not destroyed entirely, but their polluted nature, deteriorated by sin, has disappeared. "The form of this world will change as if by fire, but not its substance" (2 Pet. 3:10-13; 1 Cor. 7:31). Nothing is really lost in the world, things only change. St. John sees that everything has become new. "Then I saw a new heaven and a new earth" (Rev. 21:1). The Fathers call this the "transfiguration of the world." The whole of creation is recreated, remolded in Christ to become new. It is liberated from the vanity and corruption to which it had succumbed because of sin (Rom. 8:19-22).

The Old Testament began with the creation of heaven and earth. The New Testament ends with the creation of a new heaven and a new earth. This is the subject of Christian faith; this is the evolution in which the Church believes: God re-creates and recapitulates all things in Christ. A new world appears. In this world there is no place for the devil, for sin or for death – they have gone to the lake of fire. How in fact God will refashion this world we cannot imagine, just as we do not know how He created the world in the first place through the Logos, or, moreover, how the world will appear with Him in glory (Col. 3:3-4; 1 Cor. 15:35-38).

"And I saw the holy city, new Jerusalem, coming down out of heaven from God" (Rev. 21:2-4, 9-10). Everything becomes new. Even the Church, the New Jerusalem, is new. It too comes down from heaven, as a new creation and a gift of God. Even though here on earth the faithful are being prepared as stones for a building (1 Pet. 2:5; 2 Cor. 11:13-19; Eph. 2:20-22), the Church too is a gift of God. God gives the last great glory to the Church. Every perfect gift comes from above, from God (James 1:17).

Everything in the Book of Revelation is written for the Church. And now St. John is raised up high by the Spirit to see the Church, "the Bride of the Lamb," coming down, prepared, adorned for the wedding with Christ the Lamb. Marriage here represents the perfect faith and the perfect *koinonia* – communion of the faithful with Christ in the kingdom of God (cf. Jn. 3:29; 2 Cor. 11:2; Eph. 5:25-32). This was the dream of ancient Israel, and this is what we all desire: a close relationship with God.

The great voice from the throne confirms this relationship: "Behold, the dwelling of God is with men..." (Rev. 21:3-6). God the King is with His people. There is no more a wall of separation; no more a wall of sin that separates mankind from God. The name of Christ is Emmanuel – God with us. And the Word of God became flesh, man, and "dwelt among us" (Mt. 2:23; Jn. 1:14; Ezek. 37:27). Heaven joined earth. The Church is a true dwelling place of God in the Holy Spirit; it is the people of God, the sons and daughters of God the Father. Indeed it is only in the Holy Spirit and from a higher and more sublime point of view that one can see the Church in its divine origin and character. The voice of the one sitting upon the throne confirms this: "Behold, I make all things new... It is done! I am the Alpha and the Omega, the beginning

and the end" (Rev. 21:5-6). God created everything and everything moves toward Him as
toward their goal. "For from him and through
him and to him are all things" (Rom. 11:36).
God will have the last word in everything.
The very purpose of the world is its renewal
in Christ, the creation and completion of the
kingdom of God where God will be everything to everyone. There all the pain of the
present life will be overcome and all thirst
will be satisfied.

This renewal began with the Incarnation
and will be completed with the Parousia. At
the Second Coming of Christ, life and history
will find their ultimate meaning and goal.
Now, St. John sees these things prophetically
as events which have already taken place. "It
is done!" This is the second and final "It is
finished" (cf. Jn. 19:30) in the divine plan for
our salvation through Christ.

The Blessings of the New Creation:
The Kingdom of God (Rev. 21:4)

The old world under the devil, of sin, pain and death has passed away. Here St. John remembers the blessed life in paradise. "And death shall be no more, neither shall there be mourning nor crying nor pain any more" in the kingdom of God (Rev. 21:4). All the consequences of sin (Gen. 3:8-26) have passed away. The devil and death are now condemned permanently. Incorruptibility and immortality prevail in the new life. There is no curse, no fear of falling or of being exiled from Paradise (Rev. 22:3). But what this new life will be like in the new world, we cannot know. We cannot even understand the present life fully without the idea of the Parousia. In any case, it will be a different life; it will be a continuous worship and an immediate vision of the glory of God; it will be a life equal to that of angels (Lk. 20:34-36); a completion and fulfillment of the spiritual experience we have here on earth, where we "mystically represent the Cherubim..." In short, it will be a life of eternal blessedness and joy near Christ (Jn.

17:24-26; Phil. 1:23; 1 Thess. 4:17).

The throne of God and of the Lamb will be present; His servants will worship Him day and night. All will see His face and His name will be written on their faces (Rev. 22:3-4) in contrast to the worship of the name of the beast (Rev. 13:17). Their faces will reflect the glory of God. In the time of the Old Testament no one saw God, and the name of God was so sacred that no one even dared to pronounce it (cf. Ex. 33:20; Rev. 4:11). No temple for worship will be needed in the New Jerusalem. The faithful will see directly the presence of the glory of God and will live in this glory. The Church itself will be adorned with the glory of God (Rev. 21:11, 22-23). The whole world will be an immense temple of God, in the Holy Spirit (Eph. 2:22).

Not even the sun will be needed for light. The glory of God will light the Church and Christ will be its lamp. The Church in turn will shed its light upon all. There will be no more night, no more ignorance, no more fear (Rev. 21:23-24). Everything will be one continuous day. A river of divine grace will flow from the throne of God and from the Lamb, and it will refresh those who thirst for the kingdom of God and His righteousness (Rev. 22:1; Jn. 4:10; 7:37-39). The tree of life at the center of the city will nourish the faithful spiritually with its fruit, giving eternal life – what Adam and Eve lost in Paradise by disobedience (Gen. 3:22-23).

"And they will reign forever and ever" (Rev. 22:5). What had been foreseen in Revelation 20:4-6 will here be fulfilled to perfection. This was the purpose of the Book of Revelation: to assure St. John and the struggling Church of the final victory of Christ and of His eternal Lordship – not simply for one thousand years – but forever in the eternal kingdom of God. The kingdom of God is the end of creation that gives meaning to history. This fulfillment, of course, is through Jesus Christ in the Holy Spirit. As the Fathers say, the Holy Spirit is the glory of God and the kingdom of God. (Cf. St. Symeon the New Theologian). Now He is given to us as the first fruits and earnest of the future life, then we will have Him in His fullness (Rom. 8:23; 2 Cor. 1:22).

In chapter 21:12-21, St. John again sees and describes the glory of the Church, as external, natural beauty in its perfection.

"He who conquers shall have this heritage" (Rev. 2:7-11; 21:7-8). These good things will be inherited only by the conquerors, those who believed in Christ and struggled for a Christian life (1 Thess. 5:3-4). These are the people who are written in the Book of Life, the heavenly registry.

Christianity is a struggle and only those who have struggled well are crowned. The first victor is Christ Himself and after Him all the faithful, His army. The conquerors will partake completely of the love of God, and God will be their Father. All who are cowards in this struggle of life and death are excluded; they are relegated to the lake of fire. These people did not enjoy in the present life the blessedness of the kingdom of God (Rev. 20:5), nor will they enjoy it in eternity. Nothing impure or unholy will enter the kingdom of God (Rev. 21:27; 22:15).

"Behold, I am coming soon....Come!"(Rev. 22:6-17). A double heavenly voice confirms the truth of the vision. The angel sent by Christ confirms the truth of all that has been said in the Book (Rev. 22:6-16). And the Lord Himself confirms this: "Behold, I am coming soon... I am the Alpha and the Omega..." (Rev. 22:1-7, 12-16). At this point the Holy Spirit and the Church pray: "Come, Lord Jesus. Amen" (Rev. 22:17-20; 1 Cor. 16:22). This is our desire and our prayer: "Thy kingdom come; Thy will be done on earth as it is in heaven" for us and for the world.

When will the Lord come, or when will the

Parousia and the end of the present world come? No one knows. When the Pharisees asked Jesus about this matter, He said that the kingdom of God is within us (Lk. 17:20-21). Christ came and, in the Holy Spirit, He is always among us and within us. And one day He will come again in all His glory for the fulfillment of the kingdom of God. The only thing we need to know is how much do we have Him in our hearts; how much do we love Him and to what extent do we live with Him and in Him (Gal: 2:20). If we do not feel the presence of the King among us and within us now, we cannot expect His kingdom to come in the future. The only thing we know is that it will definitely come. But no one knows the time of the Second Coming of Christ and the end of the world. The times and the seasons are under the will of God and will always escape the scope of our knowledge. Perhaps the time will be when the number of the faithful is completed (cf. Rev. 6:11; Rom. 11:25). It may be soon or it may be in a million years! The Apostles expected the Parousia in their own lifetime (Acts 1:7; Rom. 13:11; 1 Cor. 15:52; 1 Thess. 4:17). But when it did not come as they expected, their faith was not shattered. They waited patiently, knowing that a thousand years for God is but a mere

day (2 Pet. 3:8). The life of the faithful is faith
and trust in God who rules history. The faithful are waiting patiently and always prepared
for the Parousia. The Revelation of St. John is
the history of the Church in its journey from
creation to the Second Coming of Christ (Rev.
4:11; 10:6; 22:17; Acts 1:7; Tit. 2:13; Phil. 3:20).
Faith, love, worship and spiritual struggle in
the life of the one Church of Christ, and hope
in eternity – this is the theme of the Book of
Revelation. Only such a life of faith, worship
and love can change the present world, and
not the curious observations as to when the
Parousia *is* to come, or who will live in the
one thousand year reign, and what earthly
blessings we will enjoy.

Where the kingdom of God will be – in
heaven or on earth – and what the nature of
the new earth and the new heaven will be, are
questions whose answers we will know when
we see the Lord face to face. We are talking
about God and eternity and should not ask
for precise definitions in accordance with
the standards of our present life. There is of
course need for a little flight of the soul and
of the mind, but always within the vision and
the experience of the Church. At the Second
Coming of Christ heaven and earth will be
one, one eternal Parousia – Presence of God

to men. "The throne of God and of the Lamb shall be in it, and his servants shall worship him; they shall see his face and his name shall be on their foreheads. And night shall be no more; they need no light of lamp or sun, for the Lord God will be their light, and they shall reign forever and ever" (Rev. 22:3-5). It is this eternal blessedness for which we await and work. May God make us worthy of this blessedness. Amen.

Epilogue

This is the faith of the Church in Christ regarding the final events of salvation at the end of time. This is the mystery of the divine plan of God for the world and history, as seen by faith in Christian revelation. The world is the unified work of God with a beginning, a middle and an end: Creation, Fall, Incarnation, Parousia, Resurrection and New Creation. With the Second Coming of Christ, we have the end and the fulfillment of history. Here it can be said: "It is done!" "It is finished!"

God created Adam, a spiritual human being to live a life of blessedness near God. God placed the whole world under the supervision of man to cultivate it, to enjoy it, to govern it, and to lead it toward God (Gen. 1:26-31; 2:15-17; Ps. 8:7). The disobedience of Adam interrupted the progress of the world toward God, particularly the progress of man toward becoming like God. Far from God man lost his blessedness. The world also lost its harmony and became subject to vanity and corruption (Gen. 3:19; Rom. 8:19-20). God, out of love, instituted the divine plan of salvation through the Incarnation of the Son. The Son and Logos of God became man to save His world and the free, but endangered, children of God. This is essentially the mystery of the Christian faith.

Christ, in His divine and human person and through His obedience to the will of God the Father unto death upon the Cross, overcame sin and redeemed human nature. He purified it in His redeeming death, sanctified it, and reconciled it with God. He destroyed sin, corruption and death, and brought life and incorruptibility. As victor, Christ the God-Man ascended to heaven, and as such sat at the right hand of God the Father. Heaven is where God is, and sitting at the right hand of God means having equal power and glory with God the Father. His name is already Lord of lords. As eternal King and Lord, the resurrected Christ now guides His Church militant and subdues everything to Himself, to the glory of God the Father (Jn. 17:1-5; 1 Cor. 15:28; Phil. 2:9-11). This is the special place our Lord Jesus Christ has in the life of the Church. Everything is done *from* the Father, *through* the Son, *in* the Holy Spirit. Everything in the world comes into being and moves toward a purpose, an ultimate goal, and this applies to individual persons as well as to the whole world. Everything and everyone is directed to become the Church, the people of God. The Church is the kingdom of God in the process of becoming and growing. The faithful are the army of Christ who both struggle and reign with Him. Their strength is the blood of the Lamb, the sacrifice of Christ the King upon the Cross. Their weapons are the faith and the confession of Christ, the Word of God (Rev. 12:11; 19:5; 2 Thess. 2:8).

The purpose of the Church is to bring everyone to be united with and subjected to Christ, and through Christ to God the Father. When this work is completed, when all are subject to Christ, then Christ Himself – as the mediator King – will subject Himself to the Father, "that God may be everything to everyone" of us. The whole world recreated, renewed, and recapitulated by Christ and in Christ, as one Church and kingdom of God, will be placed under the absolute sovereignty of the love of God. There the world will find the end, the final purpose of its creation. Everything will be in the love of God, in a perfect divine unity and harmony. This will be the blossoming of the seed which fell in Paradise to become a great tree (Mt. 13:31-32). The rose bush in the garden of Eden will come to full bloom. "Thanks be to God, who gives us the victory through our Lord Jesus Christ" (1 Cor. 15:28.57).

Then and there in heaven the "marriage of the Lamb" will take place, and Christ the God–Man will be King forever, sharing the throne and the authority with the Father. In the Book of Revelation, God and the Lamb are inseparable. We will see the glory of the invisible God only in the Incarnate, the *Theanthropos,* Christ Jesus, in the Holy Spirit (Rev. 22:3; 3:21; 5:13; Col. 1:13-20). And Christ, the Son of God by nature, as *Theanthropos,* will lead the people He saved, the sons and daughters of God who have become *theanthropoi* by grace. This is the depth of the mystery of the Incarnation and the salvation of mankind in Christ. God not only creates, but also saves the world and governs it unto eternity through the Son and the Holy Spirit.

All of these things have been written in the Scriptures not as a human, theoretical knowledge, but as a revelation of God in the Holy Spirit to the eye-witnesses – the Apostles: "That which… we have heard, which we have seen with our eyes, which we have looked upon and touched with our hands" (1 Jn. 1:1-4). With this faith, the Apostles brought Christ to the whole world, and the Gospel won the world for Christ, creating the Christian civilization, which the world has known now for two thousand years. The Fathers of the Church, moreover, have lived these things in faith and have embodied these truths in the doctrines, the life and the worship of the Church, so that we may always be nourished and renewed spiritually by them. This is how the Church has lived and continues to live these truths – as a religious experience, particularly in the life of worship where we experience the kingdom of God within us and among us to this day. It is, however, important for all of us, "who mystically represent the Cherubim," to know and to experience these things personally. Religion is above all a personal relationship with God, and without this personal experience of worship nothing can stand in religion. The faithful live the kingdom of Christ upon earth, but they are nostalgic for the Parousia, the end and the fulfillment at His coming again. Then we shall all be with Him as the people of God at the eternal marriage of the Lamb-Son, to reign "unto the ages of ages" (Rev. 20:4; 22:5; Jn. 17:24; 1 Thess. 4:17; 1 Jn. 3:2).

Let us not forget the hope of the "last things" at the end of time, for by doing so we also lose the very meaning of the Christian

Faith now. Faith in the Incarnation and in the Resurrection requires faith in the Parousia of the King who shall come again. It is through our faith in the Parousia – in the Second Coming of Christ, that we can also live our present faith in the Incarnate Lord of the Church, where we worship Him and await His return (1 Cor. 11:26). The present life, without its roots in the past and without a window open for the hope of fulfillment in the future, has no real meaning for man.

The Church has met and will continue to meet many tribulations in the world. Our Lord, however, has overcome the world, and in Him we can also prevail to overcome the world (Jn. 16:33; 17:14-19). Let us, therefore, not restrict our life to the present world, the temporal and perishable, and lose heaven. "The one thing that is needed" in our life is Christ and the eternal kingdom: "Seek first his kingdom and his righteousness, and all these things shall be yours as well" (Mt. 6:33). And of course the Church is always praying in the Holy Spirit: "Come, O Lord!" And the Lord affirms His coming in our hearts: "'Surely I am coming soon.' Amen. Come, Lord Jesus!" (Rev. 22:17-20; 1 Cor. 16:22).

Made in the USA
Monee, IL
30 November 2024

71694256R00062